DANGEROUS JOURNEY
THE STORY OF PILGRIM'S PROGRESS

Arranged by Oliver Hunkin

Teacher Guide
Jessica Watson

MEMORIA PRESS
www.MemoriaPress.com

DANGEROUS JOURNEY
THE STORY OF PILGRIM'S PROGRESS

Arranged by Oliver Hunkin

TEACHER GUIDE
Jessica Watson

ISBN 978-1-61538-524-9

First Edition © 2014 Memoria Press

Cover art by Thomas Cole, 1848:
Study for the Pilgrim of the World on His Journey

Contents

Introduction

John Bunyan was born in the small village of Elstow, England, in 1628. He was the son of a poor tinker (a traveling mender of pots and pans) and received very little formal education. During the English Civil War, he joined the Parliamentary Army. Bunyan moved back to Elstow after the war and resumed his father's trade as a tinker.

In his autobiography, *Grace Abounding*, Bunyan described himself as a reckless, rebellious young man. Nonetheless, after his conversion to Christianity, Bunyan began fervently embracing the teachings of Scripture and passionately preaching. However, because he was preaching without a license, Bunyan was imprisoned several times. During his imprisonment in 1676, he began to write *Pilgrim's Progress*.

While writing *Pilgrim's Progress*, Bunyan drew mainly from his knowledge of the Bible. Thus, there are many references to Bible verses and Bible stories scattered throughout the book. Bunyan also wrote *Pilgrim's Progress* as an **allegory**, a literary device that uses the characters and settings of the story to represent or express deeper truths.

Over 300 years later, *Pilgrim's Progress* still remains a defining book in English literature. It is one of the best-selling books of all time, the Bible being the first. In *Dangerous Journey*, Oliver Hunkin has used the exact words of John Bunyan to depict the journey of Christian as he travels from the City of Destruction to the Celestial City.

Comprehension Questions

After reading the introduction in the study guide and in *Dangerous Journey*, answer the following questions in complete sentences.

1. Who is the author of *Pilgrim's Progress*?

   John Bunyan is the author of *Pilgrim's Progress*.

   _____

2. Where and when was John Bunyan born?

   John Bunyan was born in Elstow, England, in 1628.

   _____

3. In what war did John Bunyan fight?

   John Bunyan fought in the English Civil War.

   _____

4. What is a tinker?

A tinker is a traveling mender of pots and pans.

5. How did John Bunyan describe himself in his autobiography?

John Bunyan described himself as a reckless, rebellious young man.

6. When did John Bunyan begin to change his ways?

After his conversion to Christianity, John Bunyan embraced the teachings of the Scriptures and began preaching the gospel.

7. Why was John Bunyan imprisoned?

He was imprisoned for preaching publicly without a license.

8. What did John Bunyan begin writing while in prison?

John Bunyan began writing *Pilgrim's Progress*.

9. What was the main source that Bunyan used while writing *Pilgrim's Progress*?

John Bunyan used his knowledge of the Bible as his main source.

10. What is an allegory?

An allegory is a literary device that uses the characters and settings of a story to represent deeper truths.

Reading Notes

settle his brains	calm his mind
wicket-gate	a gate built into a large wall
bog	wet, marshy ground

Characters

Christian	Obstinate	Help	Mr. Legality
Evangelist	Pliable	Mr. Worldly Wiseman	

Vocabulary

1. he broke out with a **lamentable** cry ___mournful, sad___
2. Sometimes they would **deride** him ___to mock or poke fun___
3. **discoursing** all the while ___engaging in conversation___
4. the Slough of **Despond** ___a state of discouragement___
5. a very **judicious** man ___showing good judgment___

Comprehension Questions

Answer the following questions in complete sentences.

1. What is the name of Christian's city and what does he learn of its fate?

    The name of Christian's city is the City of Destruction. Christian learns that the city is doomed to burn with fire from heaven.

2. What is Christian desperate to get rid of?

    Christian is desperate to get rid of the burden on his back.

3. How does Evangelist instruct Christian to get rid of his burden?

    Pointing Christian in the direction of the wicket-gate, Evangelist tells him to knock and await further instructions.

4. Name the two neighbors who run after Christian. What happens to each of them?

The two neighbors are Pliable and Obstinate. Obstinate returns back to the City of Destruction, but Pliable is persuaded to follow Christian on his journey.

5. What happens to Pliable and Christian when they fall into the Slough of Despond?

Pliable, with no burden to contend with, scrambles out and runs back home. However, weighed down by the burden on his back, Christian sinks further and further into the bog until a man named Help pulls him out.

6. What counsel does Mr. Worldly Wiseman give to Christian about how to relieve his burden?

Mr. Worldly Wiseman counsels him to seek the aid of Mr. Legality and sets Christian on the road towards his house.

7. What happens when Christian follows Mr. Worldly Wiseman's advice?

Christian encounters a fearful mountain with flashes of fire coming out of it.

Quotation

"I fear that this burden, which is upon my back, will sink me lower than the grave. Therefore, I need to get rid of it."

Who said this? __Christian__   To whom? __Evangelist__

Discussion Questions

1. What does the burden on Christian's back represent?
2. Why is Mr. Legality unable to relieve Christian of his burden?
3. What story in Scripture does the fearsome mountain and flashes of fire bring to mind?

Enrichment

Match the following characters to their representational description.

__B__ **1.** Christian

__E__ **2.** Evangelist

__F__ **3.** Obstinate

__C__ **4.** Pliable

__G__ **5.** Help

__A__ **6.** Mr. Worldly Wiseman

__D__ **7.** Mr. Legality

A. wise in the ways of the world

B. one who follows Christ

C. persuadable

D. a strict adherence to the law

E. one who shares the good news of the Gospel

F. stubborn

G. one who offers assistance to those in need

In the Appendix, begin drawing a map of Christian's "Dangerous Journey." Start with the City of Destruction and draw and label all of the major places Christian traveled to in this chapter: The Slough of Despond and the fearsome mountain. Between each place, draw broken lines to indicate the path Christian takes.

Reading Notes

fetters	chains
every tub must stand on its own bottom	an idiom (figurative expression) meaning that everyone should act independently
battlements	ramparts on top of a castle or fort
"my dumps"	a sad or depressed state of mind
gird his loins	to tie up loose or long clothing

Characters

Simple	Presumption	Goodwill	Three Shining Ones
Sloth	Beelzebub	Interpreter	

Vocabulary

1. Christian didn't **dally**. _____ to waste time by moving slowly

2. I **encountered (encounter)** by the road _____ to meet someone

3. **inconvenienced (inconvenience)** by this burden ___ to cause difficulties or trouble

4. He **groped (grope)** around blindly. _____ to feel about with the hands

5. a **valiant** man _____ courageous

6. hacking most **resolutely (resolute)** _____ determined

Comprehension Questions

Answer the following questions in complete sentences.

1. Name the three men who lay asleep while bound with fetters. Tell how each of them responds after
   Christian wakes them up.

   The three men's names are Simple, Sloth, and Presumption. Simple replies that he sees

   no danger; Sloth insists that he wants to go on sleeping; Presumption responds with the

   proverb, "Every tub must stand on its own bottom."

   _____

   _____

2. Who attacks Christian as he attempts to enter the wicket-gate?

Beelzebub, the Prince of Devils, attacks Christian by shooting arrows at him from his castle battlements.

3. At the Interpreter's House, why is there a man sitting in a dark room in an iron cage?

Although he was once on his way to the Celestial City, the man at the Interpreter's House now sits in a dark room in an iron cage because he failed to keep watch over himself and followed the pleasures of the world instead.

4. How is Christian finally rid of his burden?

As the shadow of the cross falls across him, Christian's burden slips off his back, tumbles down the hill into the mouth of a tomb, and is never seen again.

5. What two things do the three Shining Ones give to Christian?

The Shining Ones strip Christian of his mud-stained rags and give him bright new clothes. They also hand him a parchment and tell him to guard it carefully and only surrender it when he reaches the Celestial City.

Quotation

"At the foot of a hill, he passed an open tomb. Then up again, upon a little knoll, he found himself beneath a wayside cross. And as its shadow fell across him, so suddenly the burden, slipping from his shoulders, fell from off his back. It tumbled down the hill. It tumbled into the mouth of the tomb. It was never seen again."

Discussion Questions

1. What does Christian see in the parlor at the Interpreter's House? What does it represent?
2. Reread the above quotation. What two significant theological and historical events in the life of Jesus is Christian encountering? How does this affect his burden?

Match the following characters to their representational description.

___D___ **1.** Simple

___B___ **2.** Sloth

___E___ **3.** Presumption

___A___ **4.** Beelzebub

___F___ **5.** Goodwill

___G___ **6.** Interpreter

___C___ **7.** Shining Ones

A. Prince of Devils

B. lazy

C. angels

D. naïve; without understanding

E. independent; arrogant

F. kind and friendly

G. one who explains meanings

Continue to add to the map in the appendix, including the new places Christian journeyed to in this chapter: the narrow wicket-gate, the House of the Interpreter, and the wayside cross and the tomb.

Reading Notes

"thief and a robber"	reference to John 10:1
arbor	a shady area formed by trees or shrubs
embroidered	decorated with ornamental designs made with a needle and thread
passport	an official document authorizing one to travel to another country
furlong	a unit of distance equal to 220 yards

Characters

Formalist	Hypocrisy	Timorous	Mistrust	Watchful	Discretion

Vocabulary

1. he **espied** a pleasant arbor _observed or discovered_
2. the **drowsy** warmth of the afternoon _sleepy_
3. leaving Christian much **perplexed** _puzzled_
4. **chiding** himself for being such a fool _reproaching_
5. He truly feared that he would be **benighted**. _overwhelmed by darkness or night_
6. looking at him **suspiciously** _distrustfully_

Comprehension Questions

Answer the following questions in complete sentences.

1. Why do Formalist and Hypocrisy jump over the wall instead of coming through the wicket-gate? What happens to each of them?

    Claiming that the way to the wicket-gate was a long way round, they take a shortcut over the wall. When they reach a crossroads, Formalist chooses the road called Danger and loses his way forever; Hypocrisy chooses the road called Destruction, where he stumbles, falls, and rises no more.

2. Which road does Christian choose?

Christian continues walking on the straight, narrow road which leads to the Hill called

Difficulty.

3. When Christian is halfway up the hill, what does he do?

Christian sits down to rest at a pleasant arbor, and falls asleep in the afternoon sun.

4. Why do Timorous and Mistrust turn and run the wrong way down the hill?

Timorous says they are going back because the further they go, the more danger they

meet. Mistrust is unsure about whether the two lions they have seen are asleep or awake.

5. What directions does the porter give Christian to avoid being attacked by the lions?

The porter tells Christian that if he keeps strictly to the beam of light in the center of the

path, the lions cannot reach him.

Quotation

"Oh dear! I have trod the same road three times, which I should have trod but once! How far might I have been by now upon my way."

Who said this? _____Christian_____

On what occasion? _____after he goes back to retrieve the lost parchment_____

Discussion Questions

1. There are multiple times in *Dangerous Journey* where the first person pronoun "I" is used (read the first paragraph of Chapter 1, for example). To whom do you think the "I" refers?

2. After Christian finds his lost parchment, he reads words which are from Hebrews 11:16: "Desire now a better country, that is the heavenly one." Why do you think these words provide strength and comfort to him?

Match the following characters to their representational description.

<u> D </u> **1.** Formalist

<u> E </u> **2.** Hypocrisy

<u> B </u> **3.** Timorous

<u> F </u> **4.** Mistrust

<u> A </u> **5.** Watchful

<u> C </u> **6.** Discretion

A. alert

B. fearful

C. having good judgment

D. person who follows traditions without understanding

E. pretending to have virtue

F. lack of trust

Continue to add to the map in the Appendix, including the new places Christian journeyed to in this chapter: The Hill called Difficulty, the arbor halfway up the Hill, and the Palace Beautiful.

Reading Notes

pilgrimage	a journey made to a sacred place
wiles	cunning or crafty behavior
Foul Fiend (fiend)	a cruel or wicked person
"wages of death"	referring to Romans 6:23
"without more ado"	without more delay or fuss

Characters

Charity   Piety   Prudence   Discretion   Apollyon

Vocabulary

1. the mountains in the sunlight were indeed **delectable** _delightful; pleasing_
2. to share in your **felicity** _happiness; bliss_
3. born in your **dominion(s)** _territory under one's rule_
4. Christian **nimbly** stretched out his hand _quickly_
5. he, too, was bleeding **copiously** _abundantly_
6. they **staunched** the flow of blood _stopped or checked the flow of_

Comprehension Questions

Answer the following questions in complete sentences.

1. What is Christian able to see from the roof of the Palace that greatly encourages him?

   Christian sees the Delectable Mountains, from which, he is told by the ladies, he will be able to see the gate of the Celestial City.

2. Why does Christian say his wife and children would not travel with him to the Celestial City?

   Christian says that his family was opposed to going with him on his pilgrimage because his wife was afraid of losing the comforts of this world and his children were given to the foolish delights of youth.

3. What do the four sisters show Christian in the Armoury?

   Some of the objects that the sisters show Christian are Moses' rod; the hammer and nail with which Jael slew Sisera; the pitchers, trumpets, and lamps that Gideon fought with against the Midians; the jawbone of the ass that Samson used; and the sling and stone with which David fought against Goliath.

4. Describe the Foul Fiend, Apollyon.

   Apollyon is nine feet high, and hideous in appearance. He has scales like a fish, wings like a dragon, and feet like a bear. Out of his belly comes fire and smoke.

5. Why does Apollyon claim that Christian is one of his subjects? Who does Christian say he has given his allegiance to now?

   Apollyon claims that he is the Prince of the City of Destruction and everyone who is born there belongs to him. Christian says he has given his allegiance to the King of Princes.

6. Just as Apollyon is preparing to make an end of Christian, what happens?

   While Apollyon is preparing his final blow, Christian nimbly stretches out his hand for his sword, catches it, and runs Apollyon through with it. Apollyon receives a severe wound, spreads his dragon's wings, and flies away.

7. How is Christian healed of his wounds?

   In His mercy, God directs Christian towards the Tree of Life. Christian applies the leaves of the Tree to his wounds and they staunch the flow of blood.

Quotation

"Rejoice not against me, O mine enemy; when I fall, I shall arise." (see Micah 7:8)

Who is the "enemy" in this quote? __Apollyon__

Discussion Questions

1. The sisters at the Palace Beautiful show Christian many items in the armory that are referenced in the Old Testament. What do these items have in common? Why would the sisters show these to Christian?

2. How does Apollyon try to destroy Christian's faith? How does Christian respond to his attacks? What can this teach you about your own response to temptation?

3. Read Ephesians 6:10-18, in which the apostle Paul describes pieces of armor that a typical Roman soldier would wear to help Christians visualize their daily struggle against the spiritual forces of wickedness. Does this passage remind you of the armor the sisters gave to Christian? Explain why Christian is provided with armor, list the pieces he is given, and tell the purpose of each.

Enrichment

Match the following characters to their representational description.

D	**1.** Charity	**A.**	the demon of the Abyss
C	**2.** Piety	**B.**	wisdom
B	**3.** Prudence	**C.**	devout reverence to God
E	**4.** Discretion	**D.**	Christian love
A	**5.** Apollyon	**E.**	caution

Continue to add to the map in the Appendix, including the new place Christian journeyed to in this chapter: The Valley of Humiliation.

NOTE FOR FURTHER THOUGHT: After he is injured from his fight with Apollyon, Christian applies the leaves from the Tree of Life to his wounds and is immediately healed. The Tree of Life is an important motif (a recurring element in a story that often has symbolic importance) in Scripture. It is mentioned in several places, such as Genesis 2:9, Proverbs 3:18, and Revelation 22:2. In this chapter, it seems as if Bunyan is using the Tree of Life to symbolize the power God bestows upon man, so that man will not rely on his own strength and instead acknowledge God as the source of his life. Some church traditions understand the Tree of Life as a prefiguration of the cross of Christ before His actual crucifixion.

Reading Notes

apparitions	ghosts
hillock	a small hill
avenger	someone who gives out a deserving punishment

Characters

Pagan   Faithful   Evangelist

Vocabulary

1. **queried** Christian _____ questioned

2. it is every **whit** dreadful _____ bit

3. full of **doleful** voices _____ sad, mournful

4. with a **vehement** voice _____ forceful, powerful

5. he came across a **grisly** sight _____ gruesome

Comprehension Questions

Answer the following questions in complete sentences.

1. Why does Christian walk forward through the Valley of the Shadow of Death despite the terrifying warnings of the two men?

   The two men shout at Christian to go back because the Valley of the Shadow of Death is a dreadful place and they are utterly terrified.

2. Why do the two men shout at Christian to go back?

   Christian knows that the path through the Valley of the Shadow of Death is the only way to the Celestial City, and that is his destination.

3. Describe the Valley of the Shadow of Death.

   The Valley of the Shadow of Death is a dark, lonely, and silent place. The path through the valley is exceedingly narrow, with a deep ditch on the right side and a marsh on the left.

4. What is the name of the giant who tries to seize Christian by the throat? Why does the giant sit at the mouth of the cave?

The name of the giant is Pagan. He is too old and stiff in his joints to do more than sit in the mouth of the cave and bite his nails in frustration because he cannot harm the pilgrims passing by.

5. Who joins Christian on his pilgrimage?

Faithful, Christian's friend and neighbor, joins him on his pilgrimage.

6. What does Evangelist say will happen to Christian and Faithful in the town of Vanity?

Evangelist informs Faithful and Christian that one of them will die a painful death.

Quotations

"Though I walk through the Valley of the Shadow of Death, I will fear no evil, for thou art with me." (see Psalm 23:4)

"He has turned the shadow of death into the morning." (see Amos 5:8)

Discussion Questions

1. What are the three reasons that give Christian courage to go on through the Valley of the Shadow of Death?
2. Christian and Faithful have not had the same experiences on their respective pilgrimages. Why do you think that might be?

Enrichment

Match the following characters to their representational description.

__B__	1. Faithful	**A.** a heathen
__A__	2. Pagan	**B.** steadfast, loyal
__C__	3. Evangelist	**C.** one who shares the gospel

Continue to add to the map in the Appendix, including the new place Christian journeyed to in this chapter: The Valley of the Shadow of Death.

Reading Notes

commodities   goods used in trade and commerce

hubbub   tumultuous noise

sirrah   used in addressing inferiors

Characters

Lord Hate-good   Hopeful   Demas

Vocabulary

1. **descended** into the town of Vanity   moved downward
2. **contrived** to set up a fair here   plotted or planned
3. a vile **runagate**   runaway
4. **diametrically** opposite   extremely opposite
5. then I am ready to **recant**   to draw back from previously held beliefs or opinions

Comprehension Questions

Answer the following questions in complete sentences.

1. Who set the Fair up to ensnare pilgrims?

   Beelzebub, Apollyon, and Legion, perceiving that the pilgrim's way lay through the town of Vanity, set the Fair up to entrap pilgrims.

2. When the townsmen angrily ask Christian and Faithful why they aren't buying merchandise, how do they answer?

   Christian and Faithful protest to the enraged crowd that they only buy the truth.

3. What happens to Faithful after he dies?

   After an unjust trial and condemnation by the court of Vanity Fair, Faithful is executed but is taken up through the clouds by a horse and chariot to the Celestial City.

4. What happens to Christian after Faithful's death?

One of the men of Vanity Fair, named Hopeful, is moved by the testimony of the pilgrims.

While the crowd is preoccupied with Faithful's execution, he spirits Christian away safely.

Hopeful and Christian now travel together.

5. How does Demas try to tempt Christian and Hopeful? Who is Demas successful in tempting and what happens to them?

Demas calls the pilgrims to turn aside and follow him, claiming that there is a silver mine

where with very little trouble they can become rich. Although Christian and Hopeful do

not listen to Demas, the Citizens of Fair Speech are lured. As they greedily peer over the

brink of the hill, Lucre, they fall in and are never seen again.

Quotation

"For he that would by-pass this town, must needs go out of the world!"

Discussion Questions

1. After they are placed in a cage and stocks and made a public spectacle of, how do Christian and Faithful conduct themselves toward the people of Vanity Fair? How do the people of Vanity Fair respond to this? What does this teach us?

2. Why are we told that Faithful, even though he was executed, fared better than Christian?

Enrichment

Match the following characters to their representational description.

B	1. Lord Hate-good	A. a lover of the world
C	2. Hopeful	B. a lover of evil
A	3. Demas (see 2 Timothy 4:10)	C. full of hope

Continue to add to the map in the Appendix, including the new place Christian journeyed to in this chapter: Vanity Fair.

Reading Notes

stile	a step for climbing a fence
deluge	a flood of water
dungeon	an underground prison deep in a castle
cudgel	a thick stick used as a club

Characters

Giant Despair   Diffidence

Vocabulary

1. in **dire** need of him _____ urgent _____
2. an **eerie** silence _____ mysterious _____
3. a grim and **surly** voice _____ rude, unfriendly _____
4. she was even more **malevolent** than he was _____ wishing evil to others _____
5. They are **sturdy** rogues. _____ built strongly _____

Comprehension Questions

Answer the following questions in complete sentences.

1. Why do Christian and Hopeful leave the road?

   The road is rough, their feet are tender from traveling, and they are very discouraged. The shortcut across the stile seems like it has an easier path to follow.

2. Who catches Christian and Hopeful trespassing on his grounds, and what happens to them?

   Giant Despair catches Christian and Hopeful trespassing on his property. He casts them into a dark and gloomy dungeon in the keep of Doubting Castle, where they are deprived of bread and water and cut off from all their friends.

3. Name the three counsels that Diffidence gives to Giant Despair as to how he should treat his prisoners.

Diffidence counsels Giant Despair to 1) beat the prisoners without mercy, 2) persuade them to make an end of themselves, and 3) show them the bones and skulls of past pilgrims so that they will despair all the more.

4. What does Christian remember is in his pocket, and how does it help Hopeful and him?

Christian remembers he has an old key called Promise in his pocket. Using the old key, he is able to unlock the dungeon door and the iron gate, and they escape.

5. What do Christian and Hopeful place at the stile where they went astray from the road?

At the stile, Christian and Hopeful put up a notice warning pilgrims that it is the way to Doubting Castle, where all trespassers are destroyed.

Quotation

"I have in my pocket," he said, "an old key called Promise. It might just fit the lock."

Discussion Questions

1. Reread the quotation above. When we are feeling discouraged and without hope, what should we remember? What are some of God's promises that have comforted you in the past?

2. What was the Giant's secret weakness? What does this tell us about the nature of light and darkness? Look up John 1:5, 9.

3. Compare and contrast Doubting Castle and the Palace Beautiful (from Chapter 3) and the hospitality offered at each.

Enrichment

Match the following characters to their representational description.

_____B_____ **1.** Giant Despair

_____A_____ **2.** Diffidence

A. lacks confidence (in Christ)

B. hopeless, despondent

Continue to add to the map in the appendix, including the new place Christian journeys to in this chapter: Doubting Castle.

Reading Notes

perspective glass	referring to a telescope
methinks	an Old English expression meaning "I think"
Beulah	A Hebrew word meaning "marriage," It is a poetic image found in Isaiah 62:4, where God delights in bringing His people to their eternal dwelling place, just as a bridegroom delights in marrying his bride.

Characters

Shepherds   Ignorance   Flatterer   Atheist   Vain-hope

Vocabulary

1. after the **squalor** of the Giant's prison ___ filth; misery
2. the more **enmeshed** did they become ___ entangled
3. to take so **tedious** a journey ___ long and tiresome
4. Hopeful looked **aghast** at being so unwise. ___ filled with horror
5. by good **discourse** ___ discussion
6. the pilgrims went up that hill with much **agility** ___ quickness; liveliness

Comprehension Questions

Answer the following questions in complete sentences.

1. Describe the pleasant change Christian and Hopeful experience when they reach the Delectable Mountains.

   After the miserable conditions Christian and Hopeful endured in Giant Despair's dungeon, they are able to wash themselves in clear streams and eat freely of the fruit of the orchards.

2. What are the two warnings the Shepherds give to Christian and Hopeful?

   The Shepherds warn Christian and Hopeful to: 1) Beware of the Flatterer and 2) Take heed of the Enchanted Ground.

3. Why do Christian and Hopeful follow the man in white, and what happens to them?

    Christian and Hopeful think the man in white is one of the Shining Ones; they fail to

    realize he is the Flatterer disguised in a white robe. After following the Flatterer for some

    time, they are ensnared in a net and only set free when a real Shining One cuts it for them.

4. Describe what happens to Christian and Hopeful as they pass through the Enchanted Ground. How do
    they keep themselves awake?

    As Christian and Hopeful pass through the Enchanted Ground, a gradual weariness

    creeps over them. The air is heavy, they grow sleepy, and desire to stop and rest. They

    keep themselves awake by having fellowship and discussion with each other.

5. Why are Christian and Hopeful stunned when they arrive in view of the Celestial City?

    Christian and Hopeful are stunned because a deep, dark river flows between them and the

    Celestial City. There is no bridge to help them cross it; they must swim.

6. Contrast what happens to Ignorance when he arrives at the Celestial City with what happens to Christian
    and Hopeful.

    Ignorance is turned away at the Gate of the Celestial City because he does not have a

    parchment roll to prove he has come by the right road. However, Christian and Hopeful

    have their parchments ready and the Gates of Heaven are opened to them. They enter the

    Celestial City and the bells ring out with joy as they are welcomed.

Quotations

"These pilgrims now are come from the City of Destruction for the love they bear to the King of this place."

"And the bells of the City rang for joy. For Christian and his fellow had come to their true home."

Discussion Questions

1. Why do you think sleep is so dangerous for Christian and Hopeful as they walk through the Enchanted Ground? Compare this to the rest they are given at the Palace Beautiful.

2. What does the river that Christian and Hopeful cross represent? Why must they cross it?

Enrichment

Match the following characters to their representational description.

_____C_____	**1.** Ignorance	**A.** disbelieves in the existence of God
_____D_____	**2.** Flatterer	**B.** one whose hope is not in the truth
_____A_____	**3.** Atheist	**C.** lacks knowledge
_____B_____	**4.** Vain-hope	**D.** is insincere

Continue to add to the map in the Appendix, including the new places Christian journeys to in this chapter: The Delectable Mountains, the Enchanted Ground, the River of Death, and the Celestial City.

Drawing Page

Reading Notes

scuffle	a struggle or fight
ruffians	bullies
remedy	a cure
was very loth	was very unwilling or hesitant
tinder-box	a box for holding tinder, a flammable material used for kindling a fire

Characters

Christiana	Mercy	Mr. Great-heart	Much-afraid
Timorous	Goodwill	Mr. Despondency	Valiant-for-Truth

Vocabulary

1. remembering the **brinish** tears of her husband ___salty___
2. she did harden her heart against all his **entreaties** ___earnest pleadings___
3. while thus she **mused** ___reflectively thought___
4. caused the women to look pale and **wan** ___ill looking___
5. So they fell to **demolishing** Doubting Castle. ___destroying___
6. were **jocund** and merry ___cheerful___
7. the way was deep in mud and **slabbiness** ___muddiness; sloppiness___

Comprehension Questions

Answer the following questions in complete sentences.

1. Why does Christiana regret not going with her husband Christian to the Celestial City?

   Sadly, Christiana recalls the tears her husband shed as he entreated her to go with him
   to the Celestial City. She regrets that she has lost her dearest friend and that their loving
   bond has been broken.

2. Who rescues Christiana and her fellow pilgrims from the hideous dog and the ruffians?

    Goodwill, the Keeper of the Gate, rescues Christiana and her fellow pilgrims from the dog and the ruffians.

3. Who accompanies Christiana and her fellow pilgrims to the Celestial City?

    Mr. Great-heart is sent by the Interpreter to be their guardian and to guide them along their way.

4. Why do the people of Vanity Fair not stir up trouble against Christiana and her companions?

    At certain seasons of the year in Vanity Fair, a monster with a dragon's body and seven heads appears, determined to slay everyone in sight. Courageously, Mr. Great-heart fights the beast, forcing it to retreat, where it later dies of its wounds. After his victory, the townsfolk of Vanity Fair give them no trouble.

5. How is Giant Despair defeated?

    Mr. Great-heart and Christiana's sons fight with Giant Despair. The boys bring him to the ground with slings and stones, and Great-heart severs his head from his shoulders.

6. How does Christiana reach the Celestial City?

    A summons comes to Christiana, telling her to appear before the Prince of the Celestial City in ten days. After bidding her family and friends farewell, Christiana crosses the river to get to the Celestial City. The waters are shallow at the point she crosses, and the last words she says are, "I come, O Lord, I come."

Quotation

As he entered the River, he said again: "Death, where is thy sting?"
And as he went down deeper, he said: "Grave, where is thy victory?" (see 1 Corinthians 15:55)

Discussion Question

1. Compare and contrast Christiana's dangerous journey with Christian's. Explain why they might be so different.

Enrichment

Match the following characters to their representational description.

_G_	**1.** Christiana	**A.** shows a lack of courage
_F_	**2.** Timorous	**B.** full of kindness
_B_	**3.** Mercy	**C.** a generous protector
_E_	**4.** Goodwill	**D.** courageous defender of truth
_C_	**5.** Mr. Great-heart	**E.** cheerful; friendly
_H_	**6.** Mr. Despondency	**F.** fearful; timid
_A_	**7.** Much-afraid	**G.** Christian's wife
_D_	**8.** Valiant-for-Truth	**H.** shows a loss of hope

Select your favorite character from *Dangerous Journey*. **Write a paragraph of 3-5 sentences describing this character's appearance, personality, and part in the story. Also explain why you chose this character and what you learned about the Christian faith through this character.**

_____

_____

_____

_____

_____

_____

_____

_____

_____

_____

_____

APPENDIX

Christian's Map

Discussion Question Answers

Quizzes & Final (Reproducible)

Quizzes & Final Answer Key

Christian's Map

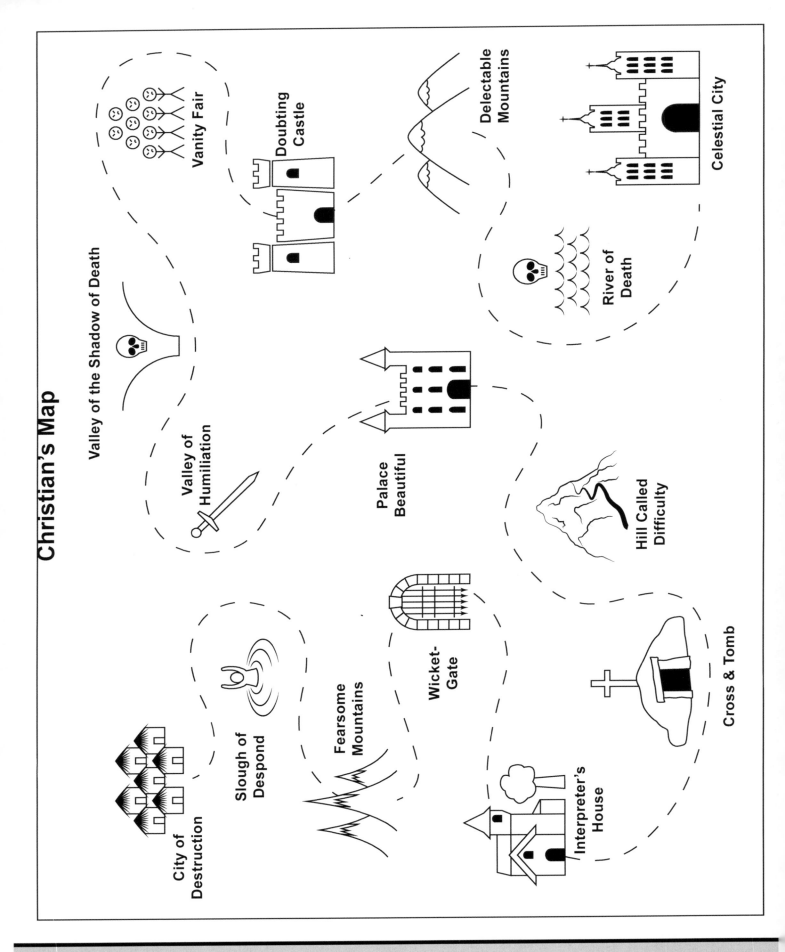

Chapter 1

1. **What does the burden on Christian's back represent?**

   The burden on Christian's back represents his sin and shame. Since the Fall of Man in the Garden of Eden, all of humanity bears this burden.

2. **Why is Mr. Legality unable to relieve Christian of his burden?**

   Because strict adherence to the law alone only condemns one further. Romans 3:20 says, "… for by the law is the knowledge of sin." The more we try to obey the law perfectly without the aid of divine grace, the more we fall short of being able to do so.

3. **What story in Scripture does the fearsome mountain and flashes of fire bring to mind?**

   When Moses read the law to the children of Israel on Mt. Sinai, the mountain smoked, thunder clapped, and lightning flashed (Exodus 20:18).

Chapter 2

1. **What does Christian see in the parlor at the Interpreter's House? What does it represent?**

   Christian sees a room full of dust. However, when the maid begins to sweep it, the dust flies and Christian chokes. The maid is unable to clean the room until it is sprinkled with water. The parlor represents the soul of man clogged with the dust of sin until sprinkled clean by the grace of God.

2. **Reread the above quotation. What two significant theological and historical events in the life of Jesus is Christian encountering? How does this affect his burden?**

   Christian encounters the crucifixion and resurrection of Jesus, symbolized by the cross and the tomb, and is relieved of his burden.

Chapter 3

1. **There are multiple times in *Dangerous Journey* where the first person pronoun "I" is used (read the first paragraph of Chapter 1, for example). To whom do you think the "I" refers?**

   This refers to the author, John Bunyan.

2. **After Christian finds his lost parchment, he reads words which are from Hebrews 11:16: "Desire now a better country, that is the heavenly one." Why do you think these words provide strength and comfort to him?**

   Fearful of the darkness around him and the lions before him, Christian is confused about what he should do. He knows that if he turns back to his own country, he will perish, but he is afraid that if he goes on, he will likewise perish. The words on the parchment remind him of his desire to reach the Celestial City, and it is that desire that compels him to continue his journey.

Chapter 4

1. **The sisters at the Palace Beautiful show Christian many items in the armory that are referenced in the Old Testament. What do these items have in common? Why would the sisters show these to Christian?**

   These items were used by Old Testament characters to slay their enemies (Exodus 3,4:1-5; Judges 4:17-24; Judges 7:15-25; Judges 15:15,16; I Samuel 17:1-50). The sisters were trying to inspire Christian to have courage to face his enemies also. As God helped Moses, Jael, Gideon, Samson, and David, he would also help Christian.

2. How does Apollyon try to destroy Christian's faith? How does Christian respond to his attacks? What can this teach you about your own response to temptation?

Apollyon accuses Christian of being unfaithful to the King. He reminds Christian of all his failures, such as when he fell into the Slough of Despond and slept and lost his parchment, and he tempts him to dwell on his inward desires for vain-glory. Christian does not try to deny his shortcomings, but simply trusts in the mercy and forgiveness of the King whom he serves.

3. Read Ephesians 6:10-18, in which the apostle Paul describes pieces of armor that a typical Roman soldier would wear to help Christians visualize their daily struggle against the spiritual forces of wickedness. Does this passage remind you of the armor the sisters gave to Christian? Explain why Christian is provided with armor, list the pieces he is given, and tell the purpose of each.

Bunyan draws from the Ephesians passage in this chapter when he has the sisters fit Christian out with armor for any assaults he may encounter along the way. Christian is given a helmet and breastplate that could save his life, a shield to fend off the fiery darts of the wicked, a sword to cut through anything, and shoes for his feet that will never wear out.

Chapter 5

1. What are the three reasons that give Christian courage to go on through the Valley of the Shadow of Death?

The three reasons that give Christian courage are: 1) Christian gathered that there were in the Valley others who feared God, besides himself. 2) He perceived that God was with them; and if with them, why not with him? 3) He hoped to overtake them and have their company.

2. Christian and Faithful have not had the same experiences on their respective pilgrimages. Why do you think that might be?

God has a specific plan and path for each individual life to take. Each pilgrim will face different temptations, sorrows, and joys.

Chapter 6

1. After they are placed in a cage and stocks and made a public spectacle of, how do Christian and Faithful conduct themselves toward the people of Vanity Fair? How do the people of Vanity Fair respond to this? What does this teach us?

Christian and Faithful behave themselves wisely, encouraging one another to trust in the Lord. They give the passers-by good words for bad. This causes the people of Vanity Fair to be even angrier with Christian and Faithful, and they demand their trial in court. From this, we learn that even though opposers of Christianity may mock and persecute us, we should "love our enemies, bless them that curse us, do good to them that hate us, and pray for them which despitefully use us, and persecute us (Matthew 5:44)."

2. Why are we told that Faithful, even though he was executed, fared better than Christian?

Faithful would arrive at the Celestial City before Christian. Having been faithful unto death, he would be given a crown of life.

Chapter 7

1. Reread the quotation above. When we are feeling discouraged and without hope, what should we remember? What are some of God's promises that have comforted you in the past?

   We should remember all of God's promises to us. Answers will vary.

2. What was the Giant's secret weakness? What does this tell us about the nature of light and darkness? Look up John 1:5, 9.

   On dark and cloudy days, he was strong as an ox; but in sunshiny weather, he fell into fits. Giant Despair represents the darkness of hopelessness and sadness, but the darkness is repelled by the light and cannot overcome it. Christ is the light of the world, who is victorious over the darkness.

3. Compare and contrast Doubting Castle and the Palace Beautiful (from Chapter 3) and the hospitality offered at each.

   The Palace Beautiful is lovely and stately; the inmates are friendly and warm; they offer Christian food and lodging and provide what he needs to continue on his journey. Doubting Castle, however, is grim and stark; Giant Despair and his wife are surly and hostile; Christian and Hopeful are treated cruelly and starved.

Chapter 8

1. Why do you think sleep is so dangerous for Christian and Hopeful as they walk through the Enchanted Ground? Compare this to the rest they are given at the Palace Beautiful.

   The sleep of the Enchanted Ground is dangerous because it means that Christian and Hopeful are not staying alert and watchful. This scene is similar to when Jesus' disciples fell asleep in the Garden of Gethsemane (Matthew 26:40-43). Although there are times and seasons when God gives us rest and peace from our troubles, as Christian has in the Palace Beautiful, we must never be lulled to sleep by a lack of watchfulness over our spiritual lives.

2. What does the river that Christian and Hopeful cross represent? Why must they cross it?

   The river that Christian and Hopeful cross is the River of Death. They must cross it before entering the Celestial City because, "he that loveth his life must lose it (John 12:25)." Scripture teaches that although we must die, Christ has conquered death through His resurrection and, consequently, death has lost its sting (1 Corinthians 15:55).

Chapter 9

1. Compare and contrast Christiana's dangerous journey with Christian's. Explain why they might be so different.

   Christiana travels through many of the same places as her husband and encounters many of the same dangers as he did. However, she often experiences greater success or victory than Christian. For example, at Vanity Fair, the townsfolk do not give Christiana and her companions the same trouble that they gave Christian and Faithful. Also, although Christian and Hopeful are held prisoner by Giant Despair for many days and barely escape, Christiana and her fellow pilgrims defeat him and rescue other prisoners. One possible reason why Christiana is more successful than Christian is that she always travels with many other pilgrims, whereas Christian is either alone or with only one other companion. Perhaps Bunyan is trying to stress the importance of fellowship with other Christians and the role of community in a believer's life. Ecclesiastes 4:9-12 says, "Two are better than one ... a threefold cord is not quickly broken."

Name:_____ Date: _____ Score: _____

VOCABULARY: Match the following definitions to the correct vocabulary word.

_____ **1.** to waste time

_____ **2.** puzzled

_____ **3.** showing good judgment

_____ **4.** to mock

_____ **5.** courageous

_____ **6.** sleepy

A. drowsy

B. judicious

C. valiant

D. dally

E. perplexed

F. deride

CHARACTERS: Match the following characters to their descriptions.

_____ **1.** Beelzebub

_____ **2.** Obstinate

_____ **3.** Hypocrisy

_____ **4.** Pliable

_____ **5.** Discretion

_____ **6.** Goodwill

A. stubborn

B. kind and friendly

C. persuadable

D. has good sense

E. pretends to have virtue

F. Prince of Devils

MULTIPLE CHOICE: Choose the best answer for each question.

1. What is Christian desperate to get rid of?
   a. his family
   b. his burden
   c. his neighbors

2. Name the two neighbors who run after Christian.
   a. Pliable and Obstinate
   b. Help and Legality
   c. Simple and Sloth

3. Who attacks Christian as he attempts to enter the wicket-gate?
   a. Evangelist
   b. Mr. Worldly Wiseman
   c. Beelzebub

4. What two things do the Shining Ones give to Christian?
   a. a map and a key
   b. a parchment and new clothes
   c. food and drink

5. When Christian is halfway up the Hill Difficulty, what does he do?
   a. He stops to rest and falls asleep.
   b. He stops to eat and drink.
   c. He turns around because it is too difficult to climb.

COMPREHENSION QUESTIONS: Answer the following questions in complete sentences.

1. What is the name of Christian's city, and what does he learn of its fate?

_____

_____

_____

2. What happens to Pliable and Christian when they fall into the Slough of Despond?

_____

_____

_____

_____

_____

3. How is Christian finally rid of his burden?

_____

_____

_____

4. What does the burden on Christian's back represent?

_____

_____

_____

Quiz 2 (Chapters 4-6)

Name:_____ Date: _____ Score: _____

VOCABULARY: Match the following definitions to the correct vocabulary word.

_____ **1.** questioned

_____ **2.** abundantly

_____ **3.** moved downward

_____ **4.** to draw back from previously held beliefs

_____ **5.** forceful; powerful

_____ **6.** delightful; pleasing

A. delectable

B. recant

C. queried

D. vehement

E. copiously

F. descended

CHARACTERS: Match the following characters to their descriptions.

_____ **1.** Apollyon

_____ **2.** Faithful

_____ **3.** Hopeful

_____ **4.** Demas

_____ **5.** Pagan

_____ **6.** Evangelist

A. a lover of the world

B. shares the gospel

C. the demon of the Abyss

D. steadfast, loyal

E. a heathen

F. full of hope

MULTIPLE CHOICE: Choose the best answer for each question.

1. What does Christian see from the roof of the Palace that greatly encourages him?
   a. He sees his wife and children following him on his pilgrimage.
   b. He sees the Delectable Mountains, from which he will be able to see the gate of the Celestial City.
   c. He sees the Palace Beautiful.

2. How is Christian healed of his wounds from his fight with Apollyon?
   a. He applies the leaves of the Tree of Life to his wounds.
   b. Evangelist comes and helps him.
   c. The Shining Ones minister to his wounds.

3. Who joins Christian on his pilgrimage after he leaves the Valley of the Shadow of Death?
   a. Evangelist
   b. Hopeful
   c. Faithful

4. How do Christian and Faithful conduct themselves toward the people of Vanity Fair after they are placed in a cage and stocks?
   a. Christian and Faithful curse the townsfolk of Vanity Fair.
   b. Christian and Faithful beg to be freed.
   c. Christian and Faithful behave wisely toward the townsfolk of Vanity Fair and speak good words for bad.

5. What happens to Faithful at Vanity Fair? Both answers must be true.
   a. Faithful is unjustly condemned and executed.
   b. Faithful is exonerated at his trial and freed.
   c. Faithful is unjustly condemned but escapes from prison.

COMPREHENSION QUESTIONS: Answer the following questions in complete sentences.

1. Describe Apollyon.

   _____

   _____

   _____

2. Why does Apollyon claim that Christian is one of his subjects? Who does Christian say he has given his allegiance to now?

   _____

   _____

   _____

3. Why does Christian walk forward through the Valley of the Shadow of Death despite the terrifying warnings of the two men?

   _____

   _____

   _____

4. Why are we told that Faithful fared better than Christian at Vanity Fair?

   _____

   _____

Name:_____ Date: _____ Score: _____

VOCABULARY: Match the following definitions to the correct vocabulary word.

_____ 1. wishing evil to others

_____ 2. destroying

_____ 3. long and tiresome

_____ 4. mysterious

_____ 5. reflectively thought

_____ 6. filth; misery

A. eerie

B. tedious

C. squalor

D. malevolent

E. demolishing

F. mused

CHARACTERS: Match the following characters to their descriptions.

_____ 1. Giant Despair

_____ 2. Ignorance

_____ 3. Flatterer

_____ 4. Christiana

_____ 5. Mercy

_____ 6. Mr. Great-heart

_____ 7. Valiant-for-Truth

A. lacks knowledge

B. Christian's wife

C. courageous defender of truth

D. hopeless, despondent

E. full of kindness

F. is insincere

G. a generous protector

MULTIPLE CHOICE: Choose the best answer for each question.

1. While Christian and Hopeful are in Giant Despair's dungeon, what does Christian remember is in his pocket?
   a. He remembers his parchment roll.
   b. He remembers he has an old key called Promise.
   c. He remembers the trusty sword he was given at the Palace Beautiful.

2. What was Giant Despair's secret weakness?
   a. In sunshiny weather, he falls into fits.
   b. His wife Diffidence is cruel to him.
   c. On dark and cloudy days, he swoons with weakness.

3. What are the two warnings the Shepherds give to Christian and Hopeful? Both must be true.
   a. To beware of Ignorance and the Enchanted Ground.
   b. To beware of Ignorance and the Flatterer.
   c. To beware of the Flatterer and the Enchanted Ground.

4. Why are Christian and Hopeful stunned when they arrive in view of the Celestial City?
- **a.** It is not at all what they expect.
- **b.** They are turned away at the gate.
- **c.** A deep, dark river flows between them and the Celestial City.

5. How is Giant Despair defeated by Christiana and her companions?
- **a.** Christiana's sons bring him to the ground with slings and stones and Great-heart severs his head from his shoulders.
- **b.** Christiana and Mercy poison his food.
- **c.** Great-heart defeats him in hand-to-hand combat.

COMPREHENSION QUESTIONS: Answer the following questions in complete sentences.

1. Compare and contrast the hospitality offered at Doubting Castle and the Palace Beautiful.

_____

_____

_____

_____

_____

_____

2. Describe what happens to Christian and Hopeful as they pass through the Enchanted Ground. How do they keep themselves awake?

_____

_____

_____

_____

3. Why does Christiana regret not going with her husband to the Celestial City?

_____

_____

_____

_____

_____

4. Why do the people of Vanity Fair not stir up trouble against Christiana and her companions?

_____

_____

_____

_____

_____

Name:_____ Date: _____ Score: _____

VOCABULARY: Match the following definitions to the correct vocabulary word.

_____ **1.** abundantly

_____ **2.** to waste time

_____ **3.** wishing evil to others

_____ **4.** mysterious

_____ **5.** to mock

_____ **6.** long and tiresome

_____ **7.** courageous

_____ **8.** forceful; powerful

_____ **9.** delightful; pleasing

A. malevolent

B. deride

C. valiant

D. delectable

E. vehement

F. dally

G. eerie

H. copiously

I. tedious

CHARACTERS: Match the following characters to their descriptions

_____ **1.** Beelzebub

_____ **2.** Pliable

_____ **3.** Faithful

_____ **4.** Hopeful

_____ **5.** Evangelist

_____ **6.** Christiana

_____ **7.** Giant Despair

_____ **8.** Great-heart

A. persuadable

B. steadfast; loyal

C. hopeless; despondent

D. Christian's wife

E. Prince of Devils

F. full of hope

G. shares the gospel

H. a generous protector

MULTIPLE CHOICE: Choose the best answer for each question.

1. What is Christian desperate to get rid of?
    a. his family
    b. his burden
    c. his neighbors

2. Name the two neighbors who run after Christian.
    a. Pliable and Obstinate
    b. Help and Legality
    c. Simple and Sloth

3. What two things do the Shining Ones give to Christian?
   a. a map and a key
   b. a parchment and new clothes
   c. food and drink

4. When Christian is halfway up the Hill Difficulty, what does he do?
   a. He stops to rest and falls asleep.
   b. He stops to eat and drink.
   c. He turns around because it is too difficult to climb.

5. How is Christian healed of his wounds from his fight with Apollyon?
   a. He applies the leaves of the Tree of Life to his wounds.
   b. Evangelist comes and helps him.
   c. The Shining Ones minister to his wounds.

6. Who joins Christian on his pilgrimage after he leaves the Valley of the Shadow of Death?
   a. Evangelist
   b. Hopeful
   c. Faithful

7. What happens to Faithful at Vanity Fair? Both must be true!
   a. Faithful is unjustly condemned and executed.
   b. Faithful is exonerated at his trial and freed.
   c. Faithful is unjustly condemned but escapes from prison.

8. While Christian and Hopeful are in Giant Despair's dungeon, what does Christian remember is in his pocket?
   a. He remembers his parchment roll.
   b. He remembers he has an old key called Promise.
   c. He remembers the trusty sword he was given at the Palace Beautiful.

9. How is Giant Despair defeated by Christiana and her companions?
   a. Christiana's sons bring him to the ground with slings and stones, and Great-heart severs his head from his shoulders.
   b. Christiana and Mercy poison his food.
   c. Great-heart defeats him in hand-to-hand combat.

COMPREHENSION QUESTIONS: Answer the following questions in complete sentences.

1. How is Christian finally rid of his burden?

   _____

   _____

   _____

2. Why are we told that Faithful fares better than Christian at Vanity Fair?

   _____

   _____

3. Describe what happens to Christian and Hopeful as they pass through the Enchanted Ground. How do they keep themselves awake?

_____

_____

_____

_____

_____

4. Why does Christiana regret not going with her husband to the Celestial City?

_____

_____

_____

_____

_____

Name:_____ Date: _____ Score: _____

VOCABULARY: Match the following definitions to the correct vocabulary word.

___D___	**1.** to waste time	**A.** drowsy
___E___	**2.** puzzled	**B.** judicious
___B___	**3.** showing good judgment	**C.** valiant
___F___	**4.** to mock	**D.** dally
___C___	**5.** courageous	**E.** perplexed
___A___	**6.** sleepy	**F.** deride

CHARACTERS: Match the following characters to their descriptions.

___F___	**1.** Beelzebub	**A.** stubborn
___A___	**2.** Obstinate	**B.** kind and friendly
___E___	**3.** Hypocrisy	**C.** persuadable
___C___	**4.** Pliable	**D.** has good sense
___D___	**5.** Discretion	**E.** pretends to have virtue
___B___	**6.** Goodwill	**F.** Prince of Devils

MULTIPLE CHOICE: Choose the best answer for each question.

1. What is Christian desperate to get rid of?
   a. his family
   b. his burden
   c. his neighbors

2. Name the two neighbors who run after Christian.
   a. Pliable and Obstinate
   b. Help and Legality
   c. Simple and Sloth

3. Who attacks Christian as he attempts to enter the wicket-gate?
   a. Evangelist
   b. Mr. Worldly Wiseman
   c. Beelzebub

4. What two things do the Shining Ones give to Christian?
   a. a map and a key
   b. a parchment and new clothes
   c. food and drink

5. When Christian is halfway up the Hill Difficulty, what does he do?
   a. He stops to rest and falls asleep.
   b. He stops to eat and drink.
   c. He turns around because it is too difficult to climb.

COMPREHENSION QUESTIONS: Answer the following questions in complete sentences.

1. What is the name of Christian's city, and what does he learn of its fate?

The name of Christian's city is the City of Destruction. Christian learns that the city is

doomed to burn with fire from heaven.

2. What happens to Pliable and Christian when they fall into the Slough of Despond?

Pliable, with no burden to contend with, scrambles out and runs back home. However,

Christian, weighed down by the burden on his back, sinks further and further into the bog

until a man named Help pulls him out.

3. How is Christian finally rid of his burden?

As the shadow of the cross falls across him, Christian's burden slips off his back, tumbles

down the hill into the mouth of a tomb, and is never seen again.

4. What does the burden on Christian's back represent?

The burden on Christian's back represents his sin and shame. Since the Fall of Man in the

Garden of Eden, all of humanity bears this burden.

Name:_____ Date: _____ Score: _____

VOCABULARY: Match the following definitions to the correct vocabulary word.

_____C_____ **1.** questioned

_____E_____ **2.** abundantly

_____F_____ **3.** moved downward

_____B_____ **4.** to draw back from previously held beliefs

_____D_____ **5.** forceful; powerful

_____A_____ **6.** delightful; pleasing

A. delectable

B. recant

C. queried

D. vehement

E. copiously

F. descended

CHARACTERS: Match the following characters to their descriptions.

_____C_____ **1.** Apollyon

_____D_____ **2.** Faithful

_____F_____ **3.** Hopeful

_____A_____ **4.** Demas

_____E_____ **5.** Pagan

_____B_____ **6.** Evangelist

A. a lover of the world

B. shares the gospel

C. the demon of the Abyss

D. steadfast, loyal

E. a heathen

F. full of hope

MULTIPLE CHOICE: Choose the best answer for each question.

1. What does Christian see from the roof of the Palace that greatly encourages him?
   a. He sees his wife and children following him on his pilgrimage.
   b. He sees the Delectable Mountains, from which he will be able to see the gate of the Celestial City.
   c. He sees the Palace Beautiful.

2. How is Christian healed of his wounds from his fight with Apollyon?
   a. He applies the leaves of the Tree of Life to his wounds.
   b. Evangelist comes and helps him.
   c. The Shining Ones minister to his wounds.

3. Who joins Christian on his pilgrimage after he leaves the Valley of the Shadow of Death?
   a. Evangelist
   b. Hopeful
   c. Faithful

4. How do Christian and Faithful conduct themselves toward the people of Vanity Fair after they are placed in a cage and stocks?
   a. Christian and Faithful curse the townsfolk of Vanity Fair.
   b. Christian and Faithful beg to be freed.
   c. Christian and Faithful behave wisely toward the townsfolk of Vanity Fair and speak good words for bad.

5. What happens to Faithful at Vanity Fair? Both answers must be true.
   a. Faithful is unjustly condemned and executed.
   b. Faithful is exonerated at his trial and freed.
   c. Faithful is unjustly condemned but escapes from prison.

COMPREHENSION QUESTIONS: Answer the following questions in complete sentences.

1. Describe Apollyon.

   Apollyon is nine feet high and hideous in appearance. He has scales like a fish, wings like a dragon, and feet like a bear. Out of his belly comes fire and smoke.

2. Why does Apollyon claim that Christian is one of his subjects? Who does Christian say he has given his allegiance to now?

   Apollyon claims that he is the Prince of the City of Destruction and everyone who is born there belongs to him. Christian says he has given his allegiance to the King of Princes.

3. Why does Christian walk forward through the Valley of the Shadow of Death despite the terrifying warnings of the two men?

   Christian knows that the path through the Valley of the Shadow of Death is the only way to the Celestial City, and that is his destination.

4. Why are we told that Faithful fared better than Christian at Vanity Fair?

   Although Faithful is executed unjustly, he will arrive at the Celestial City before Christian.

Name:_____ Date: _____ Score: _____

VOCABULARY: Match the following definitions to the correct vocabulary word.

_____D_____ **1.** wishing evil to others

_____E_____ **2.** destroying

_____B_____ **3.** long and tiresome

_____A_____ **4.** mysterious

_____F_____ **5.** thought reflectively

_____C_____ **6.** filth; misery

A. eerie
B. tedious
C. squalor
D. malevolent
E. demolishing
F. mused

CHARACTERS: Match the following characters to their descriptions.

_____D_____ **1.** Giant Despair

_____A_____ **2.** Ignorance

_____F_____ **3.** Flatterer

_____B_____ **4.** Christiana

_____E_____ **5.** Mercy

_____G_____ **6.** Mr. Great-heart

_____C_____ **7.** Valiant-for-Truth

A. lacks knowledge
B. Christian's wife
C. courageous defender of truth
D. hopeless, despondent
E. full of kindness
F. is insincere
G. a generous protector

MULTIPLE CHOICE: Choose the best answer for each question.

1. While Christian and Hopeful are in Giant Despair's dungeon, what does Christian remember is in his pocket?
   a. He remembers his parchment roll.
   b. He remembers he has an old key called Promise.
   c. He remembers the trusty sword he was given at the Palace Beautiful.

2. What was Giant Despair's secret weakness?
   a. In sunshiny weather, he falls into fits.
   b. His wife Diffidence is cruel to him.
   c. On dark and cloudy days, he swoons with weakness.

3. What are the two warnings the Shepherds give to Christian and Hopeful? Both must be true.
   a. To beware of Ignorance and the Enchanted Ground.
   b. To beware of Ignorance and the Flatterer.
   c. To beware of the Flatterer and the Enchanted Ground.

4. Why are Christian and Hopeful stunned when they arrive in view of the Celestial City?
    a. It is not at all what they expect.
    b. They are turned away at the gate.
    c. A deep, dark river flows between them and the Celestial City.

5. How is Giant Despair defeated by Christiana and her companions?
    a. Christiana's sons bring him to the ground with slings and stones and Great-heart severs his head from his shoulders.
    b. Christiana and Mercy poison his food.
    c. Great-heart defeats him in hand-to-hand combat.

COMPREHENSION QUESTIONS: Answer the following questions in complete sentences.

1. Compare and contrast the hospitality offered at Doubting Castle and the Palace Beautiful.

    The palace Beautiful is lovely and stately; the inmates are friendly and warm; they offer Christian food and lodging and provide what he needs to continue his journey. Doubting Castle, however, is grim and stark; Giant Despair and his wife are surly and hostile; Christian and Hopeful are treated cruelly and starved.

2. Describe what happens to Christian and Hopeful as they pass through the Enchanted Ground. How do they keep themselves awake?

    As Christian and Hopeful pass through the Enchanted Ground, a gradual weariness creeps over them. The air is heavy, they grow sleepy, and desire to stop and rest. They keep themselves awake by having fellowship and discussion with each other.

3. Why does Christiana regret not going with her husband to the Celestial City?

    Sadly, Christiana recalls the tears her husband shed as he entreated her to go with him to the Celestial City. She regrets that she has lost her dearest friend and that their loving bond has been broken.

4. Why do the people of Vanity Fair not stir up trouble against Christiana and her companions?

    At certain seasons of the year in Vanity Fair, a monster with a dragon's body and seven heads appears, determined to slay everyone in sight. Courageously, Mr. Great-heart fights the beast, forcing it to retreat, where it later dies of its wounds. After his victory, the townsfolk of Vanity Fair give them no trouble.

Name:_____ Date: _____ Score: _____

VOCABULARY: Match the following definitions to the correct vocabulary word.

__H__	**1.** abundantly	**A.** malevolent
__F__	**2.** to waste time	**B.** deride
__A__	**3.** wishing evil to others	**C.** valiant
__G__	**4.** mysterious	**D.** delectable
__B__	**5.** to mock	**E.** vehement
__I__	**6.** long and tiresome	**F.** dally
__C__	**7.** courageous	**G.** eerie
__E__	**8.** forceful; powerful	**H.** copiously
__D__	**9.** delightful; pleasing	**I.** tedious

CHARACTERS: Match the following characters to their descriptions

__E__	**1.** Beelzebub	**A.** persuadable
__A__	**2.** Pliable	**B.** steadfast; loyal
__B__	**3.** Faithful	**C.** hopeless; despondent
__F__	**4.** Hopeful	**D.** Christian's wife
__G__	**5.** Evangelist	**E.** Prince of Devils
__D__	**6.** Christiana	**F.** full of hope
__C__	**7.** Giant Despair	**G.** shares the gospel
__H__	**8.** Great-heart	**H.** a generous protector

MULTIPLE CHOICE: Choose the best answer for each question.

1. What is Christian desperate to get rid of?
   a. his family
   b. his burden
   c. his neighbors

2. Name the two neighbors who run after Christian.
   a. Pliable and Obstinate
   b. Help and Legality
   c. Simple and Sloth

3. What two things do the Shining Ones give to Christian?
   a. a map and a key
   b. a parchment and new clothes
   c. food and drink

4. When Christian is halfway up the Hill Difficulty, what does he do?
   a. He stops to rest and falls asleep.
   b. He stops to eat and drink.
   c. He turns around because it is too difficult to climb.

5. How is Christian healed of his wounds from his fight with Apollyon?
   a. He applies the leaves of the Tree of Life to his wounds.
   b. Evangelist comes and helps him.
   c. The Shining Ones minister to his wounds.

6. Who joins Christian on his pilgrimage after he leaves the Valley of the Shadow of Death?
   a. Evangelist
   b. Hopeful
   c. Faithful

7. What happens to Faithful at Vanity Fair? Both must be true!
   a. Faithful is unjustly condemned and executed.
   b. Faithful is exonerated at his trial and freed.
   c. Faithful is unjustly condemned but escapes from prison.

8. While Christian and Hopeful are in Giant Despair's dungeon, what does Christian remember is in his pocket?
   a. He remembers his parchment roll.
   b. He remembers he has an old key called Promise.
   c. He remembers the trusty sword he was given at the Palace Beautiful.

9. How is Giant Despair defeated by Christiana and her companions?
   a. Christiana's sons bring him to the ground with slings and stones, and Great-heart severs his head from his shoulders.
   b. Christiana and Mercy poison his food.
   c. Great-heart defeats him in hand-to-hand combat.

COMPREHENSION QUESTIONS: Answer the following questions in complete sentences.

1. How is Christian finally rid of his burden?

   As the shadow of the cross falls across him, Christian's burden slips off his back, tumbles

   down the hill into the mouth of a tomb, and is never seen again.

2. Why are we told that Faithful fares better than Christian at Vanity Fair?

   Although Faithful is executed unjustly, he will arrive at the Celestial City before Christian.

Final (Chapters 1-9) – Answer Key

3. Describe what happens to Christian and Hopeful as they pass through the Enchanted Ground. How do they keep themselves awake?

   As Christian and Hopeful pass through the Enchanted Ground, a gradual weariness creeps over them. The air is heavy, they grow sleepy and desire to stop and rest. They keep themselves awake by having fellowship and discussion with each other.

4. Why does Christiana regret not going with her husband to the Celestial City?

   Sadly, Christiana recalls the tears her husband shed as he entreated her to go with him to the Celestial City. She regrets that she has lost her dearest friend and that their loving bond has been broken.

Made in the USA
San Bernardino, CA
03 May 2015